# The SHADOW WORK JOURNAL AND WORKBOOK FOR WOMEN

## INNER WORK TO UNTANGLE YOUR EMOTIONS

# BRANDI LEE

# Introducing Your Free Gift:
# The Shadow Work Companion

Dear Soul Seeker,

Enhance your journey of self-discovery with our Shadow Work Companion! This eBook is your trusted ally, offering self-care and mindfulness practices to support your transformation.

Scan the QR code below to claim your complimentary copy and embark on a journey of inner healing and empowerment.

May this gift illuminate your path and nurture your soul.

With love,

Brandi Lee

**Get The Ebook**

# INTRODUCTION

Welcome to "The Shadow Work Journal and Workbook for Women," your compassionate companion on the path to self-discovery and healing. Designed with women in mind, this Shadow Work Journal is a safe space for you to explore the hidden parts of your psyche, embrace your full range of emotions, and embark on a transformative journey toward inner peace and self-acceptance.

Shadow Work is the brave process of uncovering and understanding the aspects of ourselves from which we've often turned away. Within these pages, you will find gentle guidance, reflective prompts, and supportive exercises tailored to help you confront past pains, heal old wounds, and reclaim power over your life.

As you turn each page, you'll be invited to delve deeper into your inner world, shedding light on the shadows with kindness and courage. This journal is designed to be a nurturing guide as you navigate the complexities of your inner landscape, offering you the tools to emerge more whole, integrated, and aligned with your true self.

# What Is Shadow Work?

Shadow Work is a transformative practice that involves exploring the uncharted territories of the self. It's a courageous dive into the depths of our inner landscape to engage aspects of our personality that we've consciously or unconsciously pushed into the 'shadows'—those aspects we might find difficult to accept. This can include repressed emotions, hidden desires, or past experiences that we've tucked away from our conscious awareness.

The term 'shadow' originates from the work of Swiss psychiatrist Carl Jung who believed that confronting our shadow is essential for achieving wholeness. By turning towards these unexplored aspects of ourselves, we learn to integrate them, harnessing their power for personal growth and self-acceptance.

To engage in Shadow Work is to embark on a journey of self-discovery where you examine the roots of your feelings, thoughts, and behaviors. It's an introspective process that requires honesty and vulnerability, as it often involves delving into complex emotions like shame, guilt, and fear.

Through this reflective practice, we can gain insights into our innermost selves, uncovering the wisdom that lies in the shadows. It's not just about facing the dark; it's also about acknowledging that within the dark lies the potential for light. Shadow Work is about reclaiming the unknown parts of ourselves to live a more authentic and liberated life.

# The Benefits Of Engaging With This Journal And Workbook

Working through a Shadow Work journal and workbook offers a plethora of benefits that can lead to profound personal growth and improved emotional wellbeing. By engaging in this introspective process, you will benefit from a structured approach to self-exploration, leading to greater self-awareness and understanding. This, in turn, can help you uncover the root causes of emotional blocks, patterns of self-sabotage, and personal limitations, which can also start to reveal a path to resolve them.

As you confront and integrate your shadow aspects, you may experience a heightened sense of inner peace and emotional release. This cathartic process can improve your relationship with yourself and with others as you become more accepting and less reactive. It also encourages emotional resilience as you learn to navigate through discomfort with grace and self-compassion.

Moreover, this reflective journey can spark creativity and unlock hidden potential as suppressed parts of the psyche often hold significant untapped energy. By reclaiming these aspects of yourself, you can channel that energy into more constructive and fulfilling pursuits.

Finally, the act of writing itself is therapeutic. It allows for a tangible way to process complex feelings and thoughts, leaving you with a clearer mind and a more grounded sense of being. The cumulative effect of this work can lead to a more empowered and authentic life, aligning your actions with your true self.

*the Shadow Work*

# How To Use This Journal:

Welcome to a personal journey of introspection and empowerment. To embark on this transformative path using your Shadow Work Journal, follow these steps:

- **Set a Daily Ritual:** Dedicate a specific time each day, even if it's just 15 minutes, for self-reflection. This consistent practice provides a foundation for your shadow work journey.

- **Create Your Sanctuary:** Find a quiet, comfortable space where you won't be interrupted. Consider lighting a candle or incense, playing soft music, or anything else that signals to your mind that this is a special time for self-discovery.

- **Breathe and Center:** Begin each session with a few deep breaths. Let the rhythm of your breathing ground you, bringing you into the present moment and preparing you for introspection.

- **Engage with the Prompts:** Open your journal and read the prompt for the day. Allow it to sink in. When you feel ready, start writing. Don't rush; let your thoughts and feelings flow naturally onto the page.

- **Reflect with Kindness:** Examine each thought and emotion that arises with compassion. This is not about judgment; it's about understanding and acceptance.

- **Close with Gratitude:** End each session by acknowledging the work you've done. Thank yourself for taking the time to look inward and for the courage to face your shadows.

Remember, this journal is a tool for growth. Be patient with yourself as you navigate this journey. Every word you write is a step towards greater self-awareness and healing.

# The Shadow Work Prompt

What are the limiting beliefs that hold me
back from achieving my goals?

_____

_____

_____

_____

_____

_____

_____

_____

_____

_____

_____

_____

_____

_____

_____

_____

_____

_____

_____

_____

_____

_____

_____

_____

_____

_____

# The Shadow Work Prompt

How do I sabotage my own success?

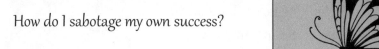

_____
_____
_____
_____
_____
_____
_____
_____
_____
_____
_____
_____
_____
_____
_____
_____
_____
_____
_____
_____
_____
_____
_____
_____
_____
_____
_____

# The Shadow Work Prompt

What are the patterns in my relationships
that I need to examine and heal?

_____
_____
_____
_____
_____
_____
_____
_____
_____
_____
_____
_____
_____
_____
_____
_____
_____
_____
_____
_____
_____
_____
_____
_____
_____
_____
_____

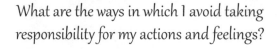

# The Shadow Work Prompt

What are the ways in which I avoid taking responsibility for my actions and feelings?

# The Shadow Work Prompt

DATE: _____

How do I use my anger and resentment to protect myself from vulnerability?

_____
_____
_____
_____
_____
_____
_____
_____
_____
_____
_____
_____
_____
_____
_____
_____
_____
_____
_____
_____
_____
_____
_____
_____
_____
_____
_____

# The Shadow Work Prompt

What are the ways in which I use my sexuality
to manipulate or control others?

_____
_____
_____
_____
_____
_____
_____
_____
_____
_____
_____
_____
_____
_____
_____
_____
_____
_____
_____
_____
_____
_____
_____
_____
_____
_____
_____
_____
_____
_____
_____
_____
_____

# The Shadow Work Prompt

How do I use my intelligence or knowledge to feel superior to others?

_____
_____
_____
_____
_____
_____
_____
_____
_____
_____
_____
_____
_____
_____
_____
_____
_____
_____
_____
_____
_____
_____
_____
_____
_____
_____
_____

# The Shadow Work Prompt

DATE: _____

What are the ways in which I avoid confrontation or difficult conversations?

_____
_____
_____
_____
_____
_____
_____
_____
_____
_____
_____
_____
_____
_____
_____
_____
_____
_____
_____
_____
_____
_____
_____
_____
_____
_____
_____
_____
_____

# The Shadow Work Prompt

How do I use my appearance or material possessions to feel better about myself?

_____
_____
_____
_____
_____
_____
_____
_____
_____
_____
_____
_____
_____
_____
_____
_____
_____
_____
_____
_____
_____
_____
_____
_____
_____
_____

# The Shadow Work Prompt

What are the ways in which I use my power or influence to manipulate or control others?

_____
_____
_____
_____
_____
_____
_____
_____
_____
_____
_____
_____
_____
_____
_____
_____
_____
_____
_____
_____
_____
_____
_____
_____
_____
_____
_____
_____
_____
_____
_____
_____
_____

# The Shadow Work Prompt

DATE: _____

> How do I use my sense of humor to deflect or avoid difficult emotions?

_____
_____
_____
_____
_____
_____
_____
_____
_____
_____
_____
_____
_____
_____
_____
_____
_____
_____
_____
_____
_____
_____
_____
_____
_____
_____
_____

# The Shadow Work Prompt

DATE: _____

What are the ways in which I use my victimhood or past trauma to avoid personal responsibility?

# The Shadow Work Prompt

How do I use my spirituality or spiritual beliefs to justify my actions or beliefs?

_____
_____
_____
_____
_____
_____
_____
_____
_____
_____
_____
_____
_____
_____
_____
_____
_____
_____
_____
_____
_____
_____
_____
_____
_____
_____

What are the ways in which I use my emotions
to manipulate or control others?

_____
_____
_____
_____
_____
_____
_____
_____
_____
_____
_____
_____
_____
_____
_____
_____
_____
_____
_____
_____
_____
_____
_____
_____
_____
_____
_____

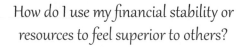 *The Shadow Work Prompt*

DATE: _____

How do I use my financial stability or resources to feel superior to others?

_____
_____
_____
_____
_____
_____
_____
_____
_____
_____
_____
_____
_____
_____
_____
_____
_____
_____
_____
_____
_____
_____
_____
_____
_____
_____
_____

# The Shadow Work Prompt

What are the ways in which I use my talents or abilities to gain attention or validation from others?

_____
_____
_____
_____
_____
_____
_____
_____
_____
_____
_____
_____
_____
_____
_____
_____
_____
_____
_____
_____
_____
_____
_____
_____
_____
_____
_____
_____
_____
_____
_____
_____

# The Shadow Work Prompt

How do I use my social status or connections
to feel better about myself?

_____
_____
_____
_____
_____
_____
_____
_____
_____
_____
_____
_____
_____
_____
_____
_____
_____
_____
_____
_____
_____
_____
_____
_____
_____
_____
_____
_____

# The Shadow Work Prompt

DATE: _____

What are the ways in which I use my physical abilities or appearance to feel superior to others?

# The Shadow Work Prompt

DATE: _____

How do I use my gender or sexual orientation
to feel superior or oppressed?

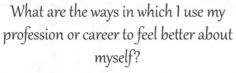 The Shadow Work Prompt

DATE: _____

What are the ways in which I use my profession or career to feel better about myself?

# The Shadow Work Prompt

How do I sabotage my own success?

_____
_____
_____
_____
_____
_____
_____
_____
_____
_____
_____
_____
_____
_____
_____
_____
_____
_____
_____
_____
_____
_____
_____
_____
_____
_____

# The Shadow Work Prompt

How do I use my relationships to feel valued
or worthy?

_____
_____
_____
_____
_____
_____
_____
_____
_____
_____
_____
_____
_____
_____
_____
_____
_____
_____
_____
_____
_____
_____
_____
_____
_____
_____
_____
_____

# The Shadow Work Prompt

DATE: _____

What are the ways in which I use my education or knowledge to feel superior to others?

_____
_____
_____
_____
_____
_____
_____
_____
_____
_____
_____
_____
_____
_____
_____
_____
_____
_____
_____
_____
_____
_____
_____
_____
_____
_____
_____
_____
_____

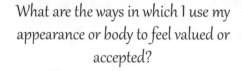

# The Shadow Work Prompt

DATE: _____

What are the ways in which I use my appearance or body to feel valued or accepted?

_____
_____
_____
_____
_____
_____
_____
_____
_____
_____
_____
_____
_____
_____
_____
_____
_____
_____
_____
_____
_____
_____
_____
_____
_____
_____
_____
_____
_____

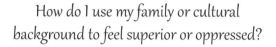

# The Shadow Work Prompt

How do I use my family or cultural
background to feel superior or oppressed?

_____
_____
_____
_____
_____
_____
_____
_____
_____
_____
_____
_____
_____
_____
_____
_____
_____
_____
_____
_____
_____
_____
_____
_____
_____
_____
_____
_____
_____
_____

# The Shadow Work Prompt

DATE: _____

What are the ways in which I use my personal values or beliefs to feel superior to others?

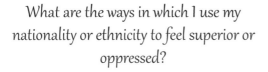

What are the ways in which I use my
nationality or ethnicity to feel superior or
oppressed?

_____
_____
_____
_____
_____
_____
_____
_____
_____
_____
_____
_____
_____
_____
_____
_____
_____
_____
_____
_____
_____
_____
_____
_____
_____
_____
_____
_____
_____

How do I use my age or stage of life to feel
superior or oppressed?

_____
_____
_____
_____
_____
_____
_____
_____
_____
_____
_____
_____
_____
_____
_____
_____
_____
_____
_____
_____
_____
_____
_____
_____
_____
_____
_____
_____
_____
_____

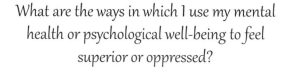 *The Shadow Work Prompt*

DATE: _____

What are the ways in which I use my mental health or psychological well-being to feel superior or oppressed?

_____

_____

_____

_____

_____

_____

_____

_____

_____

_____

_____

_____

_____

_____

_____

_____

_____

_____

_____

_____

_____

_____

_____

_____

_____

_____

_____

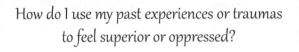

How do I use my past experiences or traumas to feel superior or oppressed?

# The Shadow Work Prompt

DATE: _____

What are the ways in which I use my sexual preferences or desires to feel superior or oppressed?

_____
_____
_____
_____
_____
_____
_____
_____
_____
_____
_____
_____
_____
_____
_____
_____
_____
_____
_____
_____
_____
_____
_____
_____
_____
_____

# The Shadow Work Prompt

DATE: _____

What are the ways in which I use my
emotional intelligence or emotional awareness
to feel superior to others?

# The Shadow Work Prompt

DATE: _____

How do I use my emotional reactions or expressions to manipulate or control others?

_____
_____
_____
_____
_____
_____
_____
_____
_____
_____
_____
_____
_____
_____
_____
_____
_____
_____
_____
_____
_____
_____
_____
_____
_____
_____
_____

# The Shadow Work Prompt

DATE: _____

What are the ways in which I use my vulnerability or openness to feel superior or oppressed?

# The Shadow Work Prompt

DATE: _____

How do I use my assertiveness or confidence to feel superior to others?

_____
_____
_____
_____
_____
_____
_____
_____
_____
_____
_____
_____
_____
_____
_____
_____
_____
_____
_____
_____
_____
_____
_____
_____
_____
_____
_____
_____

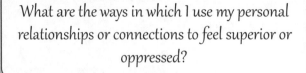

# The Shadow Work Prompt

What are the ways in which I use my personal relationships or connections to feel superior or oppressed?

_____
_____
_____
_____
_____
_____
_____
_____
_____
_____
_____
_____
_____
_____
_____
_____
_____
_____
_____
_____
_____
_____
_____
_____
_____
_____
_____

# The Shadow Work Prompt

DATE: _____

What would my 16-year-old self think of me now?

_____
_____
_____
_____
_____
_____
_____
_____
_____
_____
_____
_____
_____
_____
_____
_____
_____
_____
_____
_____
_____
_____
_____
_____
_____
_____

# The Shadow Work Prompt

DATE: _____

What are your triggers and what causes them?

_____
_____
_____
_____
_____
_____
_____
_____
_____
_____
_____
_____
_____
_____
_____
_____
_____
_____
_____
_____
_____
_____
_____
_____
_____
_____
_____

# The Shadow Work Prompt

DATE: _____

Do you feel misunderstood? If yes, what misconceptions do people have of you?

_____
_____
_____
_____
_____
_____
_____
_____
_____
_____
_____
_____
_____
_____
_____
_____
_____
_____
_____
_____
_____
_____
_____
_____
_____
_____
_____
_____
_____
_____

# The Shadow Work Prompt

DATE: _____

What do you dislike about yourself most?

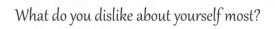

_____
_____
_____
_____
_____
_____
_____
_____
_____
_____
_____
_____
_____
_____
_____
_____
_____
_____
_____
_____
_____
_____
_____
_____
_____
_____
_____

# The Shadow Work Prompt

What's the worst thing you've ever done and
why did you do it?

_____
_____
_____
_____
_____
_____
_____
_____
_____
_____
_____
_____
_____
_____
_____
_____
_____
_____
_____
_____
_____
_____
_____
_____
_____
_____

# The Shadow Work Prompt

DATE: _____

Are you happy with where you are in your life?
Is there anything that you can do to improve
it?

# The Shadow Work Prompt

DATE: _____

Was your childhood negative or positive? Outline the most prominent memories that you have of your younger years.

_____
_____
_____
_____
_____
_____
_____
_____
_____
_____
_____
_____
_____
_____
_____
_____
_____
_____
_____
_____
_____
_____
_____
_____
_____
_____
_____
_____
_____

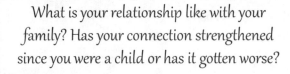 *The Shadow Work Prompt*

DATE: _____

What is your relationship like with your family? Has your connection strengthened since you were a child or has it gotten worse?

_____

_____

_____

_____

_____

_____

_____

_____

_____

_____

_____

_____

_____

_____

_____

_____

_____

_____

_____

_____

_____

_____

_____

_____

_____

_____

_____

_____

# The Shadow Work Prompt

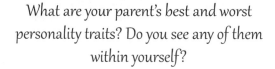

What are your parent's best and worst personality traits? Do you see any of them within yourself?

_____

_____

_____

_____

_____

_____

_____

_____

_____

_____

_____

_____

_____

_____

_____

_____

_____

_____

_____

_____

_____

_____

_____

_____

_____

_____

_____

# The Shadow Work Prompt

DATE: _____

Are you comfortable in your skin? If there is something that you would like to change about yourself, what is it and why?

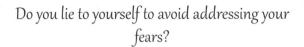

# The Shadow Work Prompt

DATE: _____

Do you lie to yourself to avoid addressing your fears?

_____
_____
_____
_____
_____
_____
_____
_____
_____
_____
_____
_____
_____
_____
_____
_____
_____
_____
_____
_____
_____
_____
_____
_____
_____
_____
_____
_____

# The Shadow Work Prompt

DATE: _____

What characteristics and traits do you dislike in others?

_____
_____
_____
_____
_____
_____
_____
_____
_____
_____
_____
_____
_____
_____
_____
_____
_____
_____
_____
_____
_____
_____
_____
_____
_____
_____
_____
_____

# The Shadow Work Prompt

When are you hardest on yourself and why?

_____
_____
_____
_____
_____
_____
_____
_____
_____
_____
_____
_____
_____
_____
_____
_____
_____
_____
_____
_____
_____
_____
_____
_____
_____
_____
_____
_____
_____

# The Shadow Work Prompt

DATE: _____

What emotions do you tend to avoid?

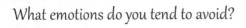

_____
_____
_____
_____
_____
_____
_____
_____
_____
_____
_____
_____
_____
_____
_____
_____
_____
_____
_____
_____
_____
_____
_____
_____
_____
_____
_____

# The Shadow Work Prompt

DATE: _____

Do you enforce boundaries with others or are you the type to let people cross lines?

_____
_____
_____
_____
_____
_____
_____
_____
_____
_____
_____
_____
_____
_____
_____
_____
_____
_____
_____
_____
_____
_____
_____
_____
_____
_____
_____
_____
_____
_____

# The Shadow Work Prompt

DATE: _____

How did you deal with trauma in the past and
what do you do to combat it in the present?

_____
_____
_____
_____
_____
_____
_____
_____
_____
_____
_____
_____
_____
_____
_____
_____
_____
_____
_____
_____
_____
_____
_____
_____
_____
_____
_____
_____
_____
_____
_____
_____

# The Shadow Work Prompt

DATE: _____

What are your toxic traits?

_____
_____
_____
_____
_____
_____
_____
_____
_____
_____
_____
_____
_____
_____
_____
_____
_____
_____
_____
_____
_____
_____
_____
_____
_____
_____
_____

# The Shadow Work Prompt

Do you accept yourself as you are?

_____
_____
_____
_____
_____
_____
_____
_____
_____
_____
_____
_____
_____
_____
_____
_____
_____
_____
_____
_____
_____
_____
_____
_____
_____
_____
_____
_____
_____
_____

# The Shadow Work Prompt

DATE: _____

What is your deepest, darkest fear?

_____
_____
_____
_____
_____
_____
_____
_____
_____
_____
_____
_____
_____
_____
_____
_____
_____
_____
_____
_____
_____
_____
_____
_____
_____
_____

# the Shadow Work Affirmations

Shadow work affirmations are statements that you repeat to yourself in order to **acknowledge** and **accept the parts of your personality** that you have been repressing or denying.

Here are a few examples of shadow work affirmations that you can use:

I embrace all aspects of myself, both light and shadow.

I accept and honor my own darkness as a natural part of my being.

I am willing to face my shadows and heal the wounds that I have been carrying.

I am strong enough to confront the parts of myself that I have been hiding from.

I recognize that my shadow self has valuable lessons to teach me.

I am grateful for the opportunity to do shadow work and heal my past traumas.

I release the need to judge or suppress any part of myself, and instead choose to love and accept myself fully."

# Healing

What positive ways can you focus on the healing process and be more accepting of your shadow self

What do I need to heal

_____
_____
_____
_____
_____
_____

Things I have healed from and how?

_____
_____
_____
_____
_____
_____
_____
_____

Things I am grateful for

_____
_____
_____
_____
_____

_____
_____
_____
_____
_____

 # Healing

DATE: _____

What positive ways can you focus on the healing process and be more accepting of your shadow self

## What do I need to heal

_____
_____
_____
_____
_____
_____

## Things I am grateful for

_____
_____
_____
_____
_____
_____

## Things I have healed from and how?

_____
_____
_____
_____
_____
_____
_____
_____
_____
_____
_____
_____

 *Healing*

DATE: _____

What positive ways can you focus on the healing process and be more accepting of your shadow self

*What do I need to heal*

_____
_____
_____
_____
_____
_____
_____

*Things I am grateful for*

_____
_____
_____
_____
_____
_____

*Things I have healed from and how?*

_____
_____
_____
_____
_____
_____
_____
_____
_____
_____
_____
_____
_____
_____

# Healing

DATE: _____

What positive ways can you focus on the healing process and be more accepting of your shadow self

### What do I need to heal

_____
_____
_____
_____
_____
_____

### Things I am grateful for

_____
_____
_____
_____
_____
_____

### Things I have healed from and how?

_____
_____
_____
_____
_____
_____
_____
_____
_____
_____
_____
_____
_____
_____
_____

# Healing

DATE: _____

What positive ways can you focus on the healing process and be more accepting of your shadow self

### What do I need to heal

_____
_____
_____
_____
_____
_____
_____
_____

### Things I am grateful for

_____
_____
_____
_____
_____
_____

### Things I have healed from and how?

_____
_____
_____
_____
_____
_____
_____
_____
_____
_____
_____
_____
_____
_____
_____
_____
_____

 *Healing*

DATE: _____

What positive ways can you focus on the healing process and be more accepting of your shadow self

What do I need to heal

_____
_____
_____
_____
_____
_____
_____

Things I have healed from and how?

_____
_____
_____
_____
_____
_____
_____
_____
_____
_____
_____
_____
_____
_____
_____
_____

Things I am grateful for

_____
_____
_____
_____
_____
_____

# Healing

DATE: _____

What positive ways can you focus on the healing process and be more accepting of your shadow self

### What do I need to heal

_____
_____
_____
_____
_____
_____

### Things I am grateful for

_____
_____
_____
_____
_____

### Things I have healed from and how?

_____
_____
_____
_____
_____
_____
_____
_____
_____
_____
_____
_____
_____
_____

# Healing

DATE: _____

What positive ways can you focus on the healing process and be more accepting of your shadow self

## What do I need to heal

_____
_____
_____
_____
_____
_____
_____

## Things I am grateful for

_____
_____
_____
_____
_____
_____

## Things I have healed from and how?

_____
_____
_____
_____
_____
_____
_____
_____
_____
_____
_____
_____
_____
_____
_____

# Healing

DATE: _____

What positive ways can you focus on the healing process and be more accepting of your shadow self

### What do I need to heal

_____
_____
_____
_____
_____
_____
_____

### Things I am grateful for

_____
_____
_____
_____
_____
_____

### Things I have healed from and how?

_____
_____
_____
_____
_____
_____
_____
_____
_____
_____
_____
_____
_____
_____

# Healing

DATE: _____

What positive ways can you focus on the healing process and be more accepting of your shadow self

## What do I need to heal

_____
_____
_____
_____
_____
_____
_____
_____

## Things I am grateful for

_____
_____
_____
_____
_____
_____

## Things I have healed from and how?

_____
_____
_____
_____
_____
_____
_____
_____
_____
_____
_____
_____
_____
_____
_____

# Self-Care and Meditation

DATE: _____

Always try to complete some self-care and/or meditation after doing shadow work using the worksheets & trackers to help you.

### Ways I can care for my mental health and well being

_____
_____
_____
_____
_____
_____
_____
_____
_____

### Ways I can care for my spiritual well being

_____
_____
_____
_____
_____
_____
_____
_____

# Self-Care and Meditation

DATE: _____

Always try to complete some self-care and/or meditation after doing shadow work using the worksheets & trackers to help you.

## Ways I can care for my mental health and well being

_____
_____
_____
_____
_____
_____
_____
_____
_____

## Ways I can care for my spiritual well being

_____
_____
_____
_____
_____
_____
_____
_____

# Self-Care and Meditation

DATE: _____

Always try to complete some self-care and/or meditation after doing shadow work using the worksheets & trackers to help you.

## Ways I can care for my mental health and well being

_____

_____

_____

_____

_____

_____

_____

_____

## Ways I can care for my spiritual well being

_____

_____

_____

_____

_____

_____

_____

_____

# Self-Care and Meditation

DATE: _____

Always try to complete some self-care and/or meditation after doing shadow work using the worksheets & trackers to help you.

## Ways I can care for my mental health and well being

_____
_____
_____
_____
_____
_____
_____
_____

## Ways I can care for my spiritual well being

_____
_____
_____
_____
_____
_____
_____

# Self-Care and Meditation

DATE: _____

Always try to complete some self-care and/or meditation after doing shadow work using the worksheets & trackers to help you.

### Ways I can care for my mental health and well being

_____
_____
_____
_____
_____
_____
_____
_____

### Ways I can care for my spiritual well being

_____
_____
_____
_____
_____
_____
_____

# Self-Care and Meditation

DATE: _____

Always try to complete some self-care and/or meditation after doing shadow work using the worksheets & trackers to help you.

## Ways I can care for my mental health and well being

_____
_____
_____
_____
_____
_____
_____
_____

## Ways I can care for my spiritual well being

_____
_____
_____
_____
_____
_____
_____

# Self-Care and Meditation

DATE: _____

Always try to complete some self-care and/or meditation after doing shadow work using the worksheets & trackers to help you.

## Ways I can care for my mental health and well being

_____
_____
_____
_____
_____
_____
_____
_____

## Ways I can care for my spiritual well being

_____
_____
_____
_____
_____
_____
_____
_____

# Self-Care and Meditation

DATE: _____

Always try to complete some self-care and/or meditation after doing shadow work using the worksheets & trackers to help you.

*Ways I can care for my mental health and well being*

_____
_____
_____
_____
_____
_____
_____
_____

*Ways I can care for my spiritual well being*

_____
_____
_____
_____
_____
_____
_____
_____

# Self-Care and Meditation

DATE: _____

Always try to complete some self-care and/or meditation after doing shadow work using the worksheets & trackers to help you.

### Ways I can care for my mental health and well being

_____
_____
_____
_____
_____
_____
_____
_____

### Ways I can care for my spiritual well being

_____
_____
_____
_____
_____
_____
_____

# Self-Care and Meditation

DATE: _____

Always try to complete some self-care and/or meditation after doing
shadow work using the worksheets & trackers to help you.

### Ways I can care for my mental health and well being

_____
_____
_____
_____
_____
_____
_____
_____

### Ways I can care for my spiritual well being

_____
_____
_____
_____
_____
_____
_____
_____

# Feel And Express

Recognize your emotions and triggers. Give yourself permission to feel even if it's not always positive. Focus on how you can get to the way you want to feel more and more each day.

### Things that make me angry & why?

_____
_____
_____
_____
_____
_____
_____
_____

### Things that make me sad & why?

_____
_____
_____
_____
_____
_____
_____
_____

### Things that make me alone & why?

_____
_____
_____
_____
_____
_____
_____

### Things that make me scared & why?

_____
_____
_____
_____
_____
_____
_____

# Feel And Express

DATE: _____

Recognize your emotions and triggers. Give yourself permission to feel even if it's not always positive. Focus on how you can get to the way you want to feel more and more each day.

### Things that make me angry & why?

_____
_____
_____
_____
_____
_____
_____

### Things that make me sad & why?

_____
_____
_____
_____
_____
_____
_____

### Things that make me alone & why?

_____
_____
_____
_____
_____
_____

### Things that make me scared & why?

_____
_____
_____
_____
_____
_____

# Feel And Express

Recognize your emotions and triggers. Give yourself permission to feel even if it's not always positive. Focus on how you can get to the way you want to feel more and more each day.

### Things that make me angry & why?

_____
_____
_____
_____
_____
_____
_____

### Things that make me sad & why?

_____
_____
_____
_____
_____
_____

### Things that make me alone & why?

_____
_____
_____
_____
_____
_____

### Things that make me scared & why?

_____
_____
_____
_____
_____
_____

# Feel And Express

Recognize your emotions and triggers. Give yourself permission to feel even if it's not always positive. Focus on how you can get to the way you want to feel more and more each day.

### Things that make me angry & why?

_____
_____
_____
_____
_____
_____
_____

### Things that make me sad & why?

_____
_____
_____
_____
_____
_____
_____

### Things that make me alone & why?

_____
_____
_____
_____
_____
_____

### Things that make me scared & why?

_____
_____
_____
_____
_____
_____

# Feel And Express

Recognize your emotions and triggers. Give yourself permission to feel even if it's not always positive. Focus on how you can get to the way you want to feel more and more each day.

### Things that make me angry & why?

_____
_____
_____
_____
_____
_____
_____

### Things that make me sad & why?

_____
_____
_____
_____
_____
_____
_____

### Things that make me alone & why?

_____
_____
_____
_____
_____
_____
_____

### Things that make me scared & why?

_____
_____
_____
_____
_____
_____
_____

# Feel And Express

DATE: _____

Recognize your emotions and triggers. Give yourself permission to feel even if it's not always positive. Focus on how you can get to the way you want to feel more and more each day.

## Things that make me angry & why?

_____
_____
_____
_____
_____
_____
_____

## Things that make me sad & why?

_____
_____
_____
_____
_____
_____
_____

## Things that make me alone & why?

_____
_____
_____
_____
_____
_____
_____

## Things that make me scared & why?

_____
_____
_____
_____
_____
_____
_____

# Feel And Express

Recognize your emotions and triggers. Give yourself permission to feel even if it's not always positive. Focus on how you can get to the way you want to feel more and more each day.

### Things that make me angry & why?

_____
_____
_____
_____
_____
_____
_____

### Things that make me sad & why?

_____
_____
_____
_____
_____
_____
_____

### Things that make me alone & why?

_____
_____
_____
_____
_____
_____

### Things that make me scared & why?

_____
_____
_____
_____
_____
_____

# Feel And Express

Recognize your emotions and triggers. Give yourself permission to feel even if it's not always positive. Focus on how you can get to the way you want to feel more and more each day.

### Things that make me angry & why?

_____

_____

_____

_____

_____

_____

### Things that make me sad & why?

_____

_____

_____

_____

_____

_____

### Things that make me alone & why?

_____

_____

_____

_____

_____

_____

### Things that make me scared & why?

_____

_____

_____

_____

_____

_____

# Feel And Express

Recognize your emotions and triggers. Give yourself permission to feel even if it's not always positive. Focus on how you can get to the way you want to feel more and more each day.

### Things that make me angry & why?

_____
_____
_____
_____
_____
_____
_____

### Things that make me sad & why?

_____
_____
_____
_____
_____
_____
_____

### Things that make me alone & why?

_____
_____
_____
_____
_____
_____

### Things that make me scared & why?

_____
_____
_____
_____
_____
_____

# Feel And Express

DATE: _____

Recognize your emotions and triggers. Give yourself permission to feel even if it's not always positive. Focus on how you can get to the way you want to feel more and more each day.

### Things that make me angry & why?

_____
_____
_____
_____
_____
_____
_____

### Things that make me sad & why?

_____
_____
_____
_____
_____
_____
_____

### Things that make me alone & why?

_____
_____
_____
_____
_____
_____

### Things that make me scared & why?

_____
_____
_____
_____
_____
_____

Made in United States
Troutdale, OR
10/13/2024

23704241R00053